A World on Its Knees

Honest Prayers in Uncertain Times

Compiled by
Madonna Therese Ratliff, FSP

Pauline
BOOKS & MEDIA
Boston

Library of Congress Cataloging-in-Publication Data

A world on its knees : honest prayers written in uncertain times / compiled by
Madonna Therese Ratliff.
    p. cm.
    ISBN 0-8198-8302-6 (pbk.)
1. Prayers. 2. Prayers for peace. 3. Prayers for justice. I. Ratliff, Madonna Therese.
    BL560 .W66 2001
    291.4'33—dc21

                                       2001006642

The Scripture quotations contained herein are from the *New Revised Standard Version
Bible*, copyright ©1989 by the Division of Christian Education of the National
Council of the Churches of Christ in the U.S.A. Used by permission. All rights
reserved.

Cover design by Regina Frances Dick, FSP

Cover photo by Mary Emmanuel Alves, FSP

Music CD production by Bridget C. Ellis, FSP

Printed and published in the U.S.A. by Pauline Books & Media, 50 Saint Paul's
Avenue, Boston, MA 02130-3491.

www.pauline.org

Pauline Books & Media is the publishing house of the Daughters of St. Paul, an
international congregation of women religious serving the Church with the
communications media.

1 2 3 4 5 6 7 8 9   09 08 07 06 05 04 03 02 01

Introduction

"Our world has been forever changed."

Nearly anyone who hears these words, lately repeated so often, would agree with them. Our world is indeed different. We now know things that previously passed us by. We fear things that once seemed far away. We long for the return of what we had assumed would last.

But one thing has not changed: we are not alone. We have our God and we have each other.

This collection of prayers for peace, gathered from people of many faith traditions and many parts of the globe, testifies to our profound connection as members of the human family. It offers the wisdom of those who have gone before us on the way of peace. And it also represents people living *now*, people praying *now*, people whose lives have been touched by recent world events and who have found themselves on their knees, searching for meaning—people whose world "has been forever changed."

A CD of peaceful, prayerful music accompanies this collection. A few selections are sung prayers; a few are instrumental arrangements of favorite melodies accompanied by spoken prayers.

Joining together with those praying in word and song around the world, may we be inspired to live a life filled with the Spirit of peace, to become people who work for peace and who are committed to living justly so that others may live with dignity.

Be Not Afraid!

Father of peace,
gather all terrified hearts
into the vast stillness of your infinitely quiet heart.
We ask this through your Son, Jesus Christ,
who calls to us clearly across the deep waters,
"Be not afraid." Amen.

    Rosemary, U.S.A.

May Hope Replace Despair

Come, Holy Spirit,
and bring about a New Pentecost
so you can rebuild
our broken world
and heal our wounded humanity.
Let justice
and peace
overcome war
and vengeance;
and may hope
replace despair.
Amen.

> Fatuoaiga, Western Samoa

Peace Is Our Deepest Craving

Father,
we cry to you for peace.
Peace is our deepest craving.
In a world of fear,
a culture of death,
a time of division,
we stand for a world of faith,
a culture of life,
a time of unity.
Take all that divides us
and all that turns us one against the other.
Change these to an unbreakable love,
an unshakeable faith,
an unmistakable peace. Amen.

Dave, U.S.A.

When We Most Need You

When all feels dark
and hope is hard to find,
remind us, loving God,
that you are closest to us
at the points where we most need you.
For nothing,
nothing at all,
can take us away from your love
in Christ Jesus. Amen.

Angela, Great Britain

Give Peace and Good to All

O Lord,
here in the Holy Land,
every day I see the devastating consequences
of injustice and hatred.
May everyone in conflict
be able to recognize where he or she is wrong.
God, inspire sentiments of fraternity and love
in the hearts of all peoples.
Grant peace and all good. Amen.

Alviero, Israel

O God, our Father, help us to realize that each of us has the power to do or to say what will bring peace. In all that we do, remove evil from our hearts. Give us hearts that seek after good and promote the progress of all nations. May your peace be close to us, through Christ our Lord. Amen.

Linda, Zambia

In Our Daily Living

Lord of the world and of peace,
help us to unite these two words
in our daily life.

Peace in the world and peace in our hearts—
this we ask of you, Lord,
for if there is to be peace in the world,
there must be peace in our hearts.

Remove from us hate and rancor
and everything that impedes
a serene and happy way of life.

Give us your peace, O Lord,
the peace that the world often
does not understand or value,
but without which,
the world cannot live.

Gloria, Brazil

Deep Peace

Deep peace of the running wave to you;
deep peace of the flowing air to you;
deep peace of the quiet earth to you;
deep peace of the shining stars to you;
deep peace of the Son of Peace to you.

Celtic Blessing

Lead Me

Lead me from death to life,
from lies to truth.
Lead me from despair to hope,
from fear to trust.
Lead me from hatred to love,
from war to peace.
Let peace fill our hearts, our world,
our universe…peace, peace, peace.

Mother Teresa, India

Remember Us in Your Kingdom

Christ,

who saved the thief on the cross,

save us from robbing and exploiting

our fellow human beings.

Author Unknown

Blessed are the peacemakers,
for they will be called children of God.

Matthew 5:9

Take Care of Our Family

God, praying for peace means so much more now that we have children. We've had to become less centered on ourselves and more aware of how the events happening in the world affect us as a family.

Lord, we pray for peace in our home and in homes everywhere. We pray that you will grant peace to the whole world— one heart at a time.

Kara and Brian, U.S.A.

Do Not Leave Us Hopeless

Father God,
our hearts are gripped with mixed emotions and helplessness
in the face of a faceless enemy—terrorism.
Lord, send the light of your Spirit
to remove the blindness and darkness
that has engulfed our hearts and minds,
and open our own spirits to know your wisdom.
By the saving power of the cross,
guide our thoughts and actions.
Jesus, Wounded Healer, Prince of Peace,
let us not give in to hopelessness and fear. Amen.

Zeny, Philippines

How Can I Forgive?

Lord—how am I to react?
Didn't Jesus teach us to love our enemies
and to do good to those who hate us,
to love our friends
and pray for our enemies, to forgive?
Yet, how am I to accomplish this? Help me, Lord!

Jen, U.S.A.

We Are Deeply Affected

Lord, we are deeply affected by the lack of peace around us.
We live our daily lives entrapped by age, race, sex, caste,
and class. Our life is choked off by the separation of people
from one another, and by hatred that leads to war.

The universal cry of broken humanity is "Peace."

We believe that you are the Lord of peace and love. Help us to
accept the shortcomings of each one and to forgive and forget the
wrong done to one another. Thus, peace and love may reign
in our world and we may be able to live as brothers and sisters.

Aley, India

"Peace!" shall be the word spoken by a merciful God.

Qur'an 36:58

Radiating Peace

God of all goodness and love,
we thank and praise you
because you desire all creation to live in harmony.
Re-enkindle this harmony
in the heart of each one of us
regardless of our nationality or race;
allow us to collaborate with you
in bringing peace and tranquility.

Let us live and share that peace which comes from you,
not from any human invention.
May our lives radiate peace to all. Amen.

Susan, Kenya

Prayer for Passover

We stand on sacred ground,
before the burning bush,
in awe and our shoes removed.
May we always remember that burning bush
in our hearts and act justly wherever we go.

Author Unknown

Purge the Violence!

Lord God, you are the source of peace. Grant that we may give witness to your justice and peace. Hear our prayer and grant us strength so that we may respond to hatred with love, to injustice with total dedication to justice, to war with peace.

Heal with your love the brokenness and deteriorating situation of our nation, ravaged by violence, crimes, draught, and disease, especially AIDS.

Give us the grace to purge ourselves of all violence in our own thoughts and actions, in our family life, in our friendships, and in our relationships.

Fill us with your Spirit, that we may follow Jesus the way, the truth, and the life in all we do or say, working for justice and bringing your peace to this land.

O God, hear our prayer and grant the world your everlasting peace. Amen.

Paula, South Africa

You Are Within Us

Lord,
let us light our candles,
but may our light
come from that place
within our hearts
that melts the source
of terror and wrong. Amen.

Margaret, U.S.A.

"Where Were You, God, on September 11?"

God's voice echoes in the darkness:

"I know you're angry with me right now. That's all right. It's all right to be angry over injustice. Getting angry is part of being human. Remember, Jesus became angry, too!

"'Where were you, God?' you demand. And I answer, I was *there*. I whispered in the ear of a little girl, 'Don't be afraid, I am with you.' I held the hand of a business woman as tightly as she clutched mine. I cradled a pilot against my shoulder as if he were a baby again.

"Amid the paralyzing fear, I was there, as I was there with my Son in the garden. Amid the unbearable pain, I was there. Amid the terrible realization that life was ending too soon, I was there as he hung on the cross and asked, like you, 'My God, my God…why have you forsaken me?'

"I had not forsaken *him,* and I did not forsake *them*.

"In an instant, they came into existence. In an instant, they left this world. But even in that last instant, I kept my promise: I am with you—*always*."

Author Unknown

A Call to Those Who Lead

The world would have peace if those involved in politics would only follow the Gospel.

Saint Bridget of Sweden

We Are Numb with Grief

Dear Lord,
the numbness
still remains,
the memories play and
replay in our minds.
We go through the motions,
but nothing has the same
meaning anymore.
With lives destroyed,
is there now *un*meaning?

Yet, I sense a new spirit,
a solidarity of soul,
a reaching out of hands.
We seem united
and consoled by this unity.

Thank you, Lord. Amen.

Benedict, U.S.A.

Come to Our Broken Relationships

Jesus Christ, teach us your new justice and unite us into one.

Holy Spirit, touch the hearts of those who have power.

Let them realize the greatness of the responsibility

they have taken upon themselves,

and lead them to set right the broken relationships

between people and nations.

May they turn all their strength and ability

toward creating a better world,

which provides sufficiently for all people on earth. Amen.

Someone praying in the Czech Republic

May We Focus on Peace

To Allah, the Great, the Merciful, the Compassionate:
We will only have the kind of peace that you want
if you help us to accomplish it.
A wounded, war-filled life
is far from your plan.
May we focus on peace
more than anything else. Salaam.

Mohammad, Afghanistan

We Belong to Each Other

Lord God, thank you for reminding us of what's truly important in life. Seeing the entire world come together as your family is so inspiring—we often forget that we are accountable for our neighbor, regardless of the distance or difference. Lord, trials bring us closer to one another in spirit. Continue to sustain this unity under your umbrella of love. Amen.

Thelma, Philippines

No Words

Lord—
I am speechless in the face of tragedy.
I pray:
have mercy on us all
and bring us to eternal life.
Amen.

Alison, U.S.A.

Your Peace Floods Us

Jesus,

at this moment, please come to us.

Let your peace grow in us

so anger, grief, confusion, and hate

can no longer take control.

You are our Way, our Truth, and our Life—

the Way to forgive and to love even our enemy;

the Truth we live by when we follow your words;

the Life that leads to eternal life with you.

We close our eyes,

breathe deeply,

and remember that you, Jesus, gave your life for us.

Now your light shines through us

and the darkness is vanished.

Your love embraces us,

and your peace floods us.

We are now at peace,

for you are with us.

Phivan, Vietnam

May the Lord give strength to his people!
May the Lord bless his people with peace!

Psalm 29:11

Children Want Peace, Not War

Dear Lord,
I feel the hurt that everyone feels
when seeing violence and hatred.
You always listen to our prayers—
help us not to be afraid of tomorrow.
I know that the children who have died in tragic events
are in heaven with you.
All of us children want peace, not war.
Thank you, Lord, for hearing me.
I pray with lots of love. Amen.

Marcella, 13 years old, El Salvador

Our Divided World

Heavenly Father, God of justice and peace,
you created us in your image and you created us free.
Help all people to use their freedom for the good of all.
May all feel the great need of peace in our divided world.
May all work for justice which gives rise to peace,
and may we realize that in our differences lies our strength,
in our diversity lies our unity,
and that, though we speak different tongues,
we are one people under one Father,
through Christ our Lord. Amen.

Chy Chy and Em Em, Nigeria

Peace Flows from You

God, source of eternal peace,
make us receptive to the peace that flows from you.
Both the world and the people you created
have never given enough attention
to what you offered when you said,
"Peace I give to you, my peace I leave with you."

Joeyanna, India

Let Me Embrace Others' Pain

Lord, grant me a listening heart
open to your concerns,
open to others' needs.
Give me a large heart that embraces all people
of every culture throughout the world.

Reconcile people to yourself and to one another.
Heal wounds: physical, emotional, and spiritual.
Give everyone what is needed for survival in this world.

Deepen our awareness
that because you made us for yourself
our hearts will always be restless.

May all of us grow in love for you and one another,
so that we may build a new earthly city...
while we await the eternal city of heaven. Amen.

Mary Elizabeth, U.S.A.

The Day of Peace

I am falling everywhere;
I am searching the whole world
for what I found a long time ago.
I will never forget how it gave me a little hope.
Will I ever find it again?
It was a shower on our life,
but it seems lost.
Everything seems lost:
joy, love, hope, and care.
I search for a day of peace;
it is really peace that we need.

Shagufta, Pakistan

Yesterday, Lord, my innocence died.
I wonder if I'll ever remember peace.
I pray for the thousands of innocent
and I pray for the handful of guilty,
and I know that God is with us all.
I cry for the thousands and I cry at the handful,
and I know that God is comforting us.
I send my love to the thousands and I think of the handful…
and I accept that God loves us all.
I believe you and I believe *in* you.
I pray for healing; I want to find peace.

    Tammy, U.S.A.

Giver of Peace

Allah is God, besides whom there is no other.

He is the sovereign Lord,

the Holy One,

the Giver of Peace,

the Keeper of Faith;

the Guardian,

the Mighty One,

the All-Powerful,

the Most High! Exalted be God!

Qur'an 59:23

Solidarity of the Human Family

God,

we are all brothers and sisters,

no matter our nationality.

You want us to love one another in solidarity.

We are united, despite our language, our faith, our country,

when we are united in pain.

But as your children, we are also united in one hope,

and in love shown in deeds.

Today we pray for our suffering brothers and sisters

around the world,

that they might be able to trust in you,

who can create everything anew.

Bless us and strengthen us always. Amen.

Maria, Columbia

We Are Scared

God,

we are scared.

Help us not to hurt people.

How can we help the poor kids?

Thank you for our family and friends. Amen.

Good Shepherd School, kindergarten class, U.S.A.

Let Love Shine in Us

Lord Jesus,
you know all things,
especially the depth of our hearts.
I plead for our world,
often darkened by hate, envy, and rancor.
Let your love and your light shine in us
that we might learn how to love one another
as brothers and sisters—
children of God our Father. Amen.

Roberto, El Salvador

Give Us Our Daily Bread

Loving Creator of all things,
God of all people,
our comfort and our hope,
your people of all faiths, of uncertain faith,
even those who have not known you
and do not know you still,
are shocked and wounded
by the touch of sudden death and destruction
that has reached new and unexpected quarters,
new and unimagined dimensions.

In times of pain, confusion, and deep loss,
you stir in the heart of humanity,
around the globe,
a common grief.
We mourn the loss of life, the suffering,
but also our lost innocence,
our preoccupation with simple things
perhaps so daunting once,
but now so very, very small.

In this time when the children of your love are united,
help us to stitch the human family
back together in love and peace—
a peace that must flow from your justice.

Let us be mindful of all members of the human family,
and of the justice *all* of them are due,
that the unity forged in sorrow may produce
the flowering of your kingdom,
where all of us, your children everywhere,
will receive our daily bread,
will have a safe place to rest,
and will know the great gift
that each of us is intended to be to this world,
because you made us to be gift. Amen.

Scott, U.S.A.

That We May See!

An eye for an eye makes the whole world blind.

Mahatma Gandhi, India

Hold Our Pain

Dear Lord,
I hold in my heart all the pain
that has been experienced throughout the world.
Grant eternal rest to those who have died in disasters,
those who were fathers and mothers,
those who were teenagers and children,
aunts and uncles, grandparents, and beloved friends.
From heaven, may they bless us and preserve us
from the hate and injustice that unleashes war.
Listen to my prayer, Lord. I offer it with all my heart. Amen.

Ana Frida, El Salvador

Seek Peace

Depart from evil and do good; seek peace and pursue it. The eyes of the Lord are on the righteous, and his ears are open to their cry.

Psalm 34:14–15

Make the World Better

Hear me, O Lord…I cry to you for help. I ask for the strength to stand strong, for the humility to speak the truth with compassion. Help me to understand the pain that my brother, my sister, my neighbor, my child may be experiencing, so that I will be tolerant, helpful, honest, and true.

Grant me the inner love to share my heart and to nurture others. Fill me with your Spirit so that I may walk in faith and make this world a better place, if only for a moment. Amen.

Akicita, Canada

Do It Now, Lord!

At this point in our lives, we turn to you, God our Father.

Your word says, "I will take away your stony hearts and give you hearts of love." This is our need in this hour. Lord, we ask you to do this for us, and do it now. Reconcile us to one another. Amen.

Livia, India

Our Hearts Are Filled with Loss

Lord,

how could this have happened?

You are the Creator God.

Many call you Allah, others Yahweh, Abba, Father.

You are the one God who brings life and peace to your children,

not death and fear.

Have mercy on us.

Our hearts are filled with love and loss;

don't let hatred turn our hearts to stone.

Bring us peace in your wide arms of mercy.

Gather us all together as your children.

May we see you in one another's eyes.

Have mercy on us, dear God.

Grant us peace. Amen.

Mary Margaret, U.S.A.

Human Dignity in Everything

Progress is not only concerned with feeding and clothing humanity, or expanding agricultural methods with the sinking of wells or the digging of canals. It also means the promotion of human dignity in every way so that all people may live in a manner more befitting their dignity.

F. X. Nguyen Van Thuan, Vietnam

For God is a God not
of disorder
but of peace.

1 Corinthians 14:33

God, What's Going On?

When symbols of power have collapsed,
and lives of innocents
have been senselessly crushed out,
and the world stands silent in horrified shock...
God, what is going on?
We're afraid.

And yet, all is possible with you, isn't it?
So in disasters bigger than life itself,
we will not be overcome.
You are bigger than the death that is generated
by what is darkest in us.
You bring life out of our deaths.

Show us how to be life, too,
in the face of this death.
Make us hope and peace. Amen.

Chris, Germany

Crucifixion of the World

Jesus, I watched on the news how the people of Afghanistan, particularly the women, are oppressed. They risk their lives just to go to school; they cannot go out alone in public, and must always be entirely covered. They cannot hold jobs to provide for their families. They are cut off from the outside world.

I look at the crucifix hanging on the wall and wonder what you would have us do. You can't desire that your people live in oppression, unable to love freely and be treated without dignity!

My Afghani sisters are poor, and even their basic needs for food, family, and doctors are neglected. They are killed easily at an oppressor's whim! To them, Jesus, I want to shout your words, "I AM WITH YOU." Your presence here with these suffering women—this is where the cross makes some sort of "sense"!

Bring us peace in your cross, and grant us your Spirit as we speak and act. Give us strength to claim freedom and not to fear death, knowing that you have something greater in store for us. Give us courage; make us free. And let us live what is so easily prayed!

Donna Jean, U.S.A.

The Kiss of Justice and Peace

Steadfast love and faithfulness will meet; righteousness and peace will kiss each other. Faithfulness will spring up from the ground, and righteousness will look down from the sky.

Psalm 85:10–11

May Peace Flow Like Rain

*"I will extend peace to her like a river, and
the honor of nations like a flowing stream"* (Is 66:12).

Let us ask of the Wellspring of Peace:
may it flow like the dew,
may peace drop like the rain,
until the earth is filled with peace
as the waters cover the sea.

The Birkat Shalom

O Peaceful God: A Muslim Supplication

O all-loving God,
help all of us recognize our human kinship to each other
and instill your love in our hearts.

O God of protection,
show all faithful people the way to protect each and every human
life from acts of brutality and inhumanity.

O God of unity,
we pray that you help Muslims, Christians, Jews, and all people
of faith to unite against all sources of evil and take a firm stand
against enmity, hatred, injustice, and divisiveness.

O God who is truth and light,
let the truth of your message of peace bring the light of wisdom
and patience to all our hearts.

O God all-wise,
plant the seeds of true wisdom in each of our hearts so that we
may come to truly love and respect each other as you teach us to
do through your prophets and revelations.

O God of hope,

remind us that hope is like a determined flower, springing up to
full bloom even in the harshest environment. We must always
remain hopeful that truth, justice, mutual love, and respect
will prevail, despite the efforts of those who conspire against it.
For your mercy and justice are everlasting. Amen.

Noha, Egypt

So High, So Deep, So Wide

Heavenly Father,
heed the plea of your children for peace and sanity in the world!
Your love for us, your human creation, is so good, so great, so
perfect, that it can never fail us. It is, therefore, to you and
to you alone that we can turn. Your love for us is so high
that we can't get over it! So deep that we can't get beneath,
so wide we just can't get around it! We beg of you, Father,
to let the power of your love rightfully hold sway
over our hearts, our minds, our very being.

Ladislaus, India

A Blow to the Heart

I ache for the world,
yearn for peace,
cry for the pain.
A blow to the center,
a blow to our hearts.
When one is pained,
we *all* are pained,
united in spirit,
not in nationality.
One is hurt, we all hurt.
because no "they" or "us" exists.

> We love…
>> We weep…
>>> We hope…

Amy, U.S.A.

Upset Our Easiness

If you were content, Lord,
you would not bother with us.
But you are restless:
through anger, through excitement, and through love,
you will all things to change and be made new.

So we praise you
that your restlessness has been born in us:
as the pain of the world,
the cries of your people,
the urgency of your gospel,
and your Holy Spirit
upset our easiness
and require us to respond.

Someone praying in Scotland

May Your Gentle Hand Brush Away My Tears

Gentle God,

help me not so much to understand what has happened

as to accept and continue to live my life,

filled with love and compassion.

As your gentle hand softly wipes away my tears,

let me not turn from you and your ways, but *to* you.

Let me pour out the anger and despair overwhelming my heart

so that you may fill me with peace and charity.

Help me, Lord,

to turn these hands of mine into your hands,

that I may be your gentle touch

for someone who may need it,

your voice for someone

who longs for your encouragement,

and your heart to love all men and women. Amen.

Marlyn, Costa Rica

Send Your Peace

Send your peace, O Lord, which is perfect and everlasting,
that our souls may radiate peace.

Send your peace, O Lord,
that we may think, act, and speak harmoniously.

Send your peace, O Lord,
that we may be contented and thankful for your bountiful gifts.

Send your peace, O Lord, amidst our worldly strife,
that we may enjoy your bliss.

Send your peace, O Lord,
that we may endure all, tolerate all,
in the thought of your grace and mercy.

Send your peace, O Lord,
that our lives may become a divine vision,
and in your light all darkness may vanish.

Send your peace, O Lord, our Father and Mother,
that we your children on earth may all unite in one family.

Hazrat Inayat Khan, India

Sixth-Century Peace Prayer

If there is to be peace in the world,
there must be peace in the nations.

If there is to be peace in the nations,
there must be peace in the cities.

If there is to be peace in the cities,
there must be peace between neighbors.

If there is to be peace between neighbors,
there must be peace in the home.

Lao-tse, China

Help Me Trust in the Darkness

Thank you, Lord, for everything—for my life and those you have given to me. Please keep everyone I love safe!

Lord, help me to recognize you in all the "disguises" you wear, so that I never fail to feed the hungry, comfort the ill, visit the prisoners. I know I was sent here to be a blazing spark of your love, to help you in your ever-continuing expression of creation. Keep my eyes and heart open so that I never fail to gasp at the wonder and beauty of your creation.

I want to always trust you, even when I don't understand why you sometimes seem to have disappeared. Help me in dark times to remember that the other side of the cross is rebirth. I trust you in everything. Amen.

Antoinette, U.S.A.

Give Us Forgiving Hearts

O Lord, send your Spirit to the world and make it better. Give us that peace which the world cannot give. There is a call for peace, a longing for love and harmony. Grant us the heart to forgive everyone.

Lord, you see that the world is surrounded by evil,
> corruption,
>> selfishness,
>>> pride.

Give us the courage to turn them into kindness,
> harmony,
>> love,
>>> forgiveness.

May we build a foundation of peace to promote justice,
> truth,
>> charity,
>>> freedom.

May we all contribute to making this foundation strong.

This is my prayer, which I make through Christ our Lord. Amen.

Rubina, Pakistan

Icon of Love

Lord Jesus,
as we look at our world
with its anguish and its fears,
we realize that we are all vulnerable,
prisoners of ambiguity,
prisoners of those more powerful than us,
prisoners of a profound malaise
which has overshadowed the history of the world.

We lift our hands toward you
in this nighttime of war.
We are afraid,
but we want to remain firm
in the certainty that a new day will arrive,
because you, Lord, are always Light
even when all else is dark and dim.

Lord, you who overcame violence and death
for the life of the world,
help us to live for peace.

May each of us carry within ourselves
all of humanity,
as a living icon of your love.
May peace become our home
and may we live in the joy of your resurrection.

Agnese, Italy

Show Us the Way!

In the Name of God, the Compassionate, the Most Merciful:
All praise belongs to God,
Lord of all worlds,
the Compassionate, the Merciful,
Ruler of Judgment Day.
It is you that we worship,
and to you we appeal for help.
Show us the straight way,
the way of those you have graced,
not of those on whom is your wrath,
nor of those who wander astray.

Qur'an 1:1–9

You

You are the peace of all things calm,
you are the place to hide from harm,
you are the light that shines in dark,
you are the heart's eternal spark,
you are the door that's open wide,
you are the guest who waits inside,
you are the stranger at the door,
you are the calling of the poor,
you are the light, the truth, the way,
you are my Savior this very day.

Ancient Celtic blessing

Making Love Practical

O God, we pray for all those in our world who are suffering from injustice: for those who are discriminated against because of their race, color, or religion; for those imprisoned for working for the relief of oppression; for those who are hounded for speaking the inconvenient truth; for those tempted to violence as a cry against overwhelming hardship; for those deprived of reasonable health and education; for those suffering from hunger and famine; for those too weak to help themselves and who have no one else to help them; for the unemployed who cry out for work, but do not find it.

We pray for anyone of our acquaintance who is personally affected by injustice. Forgive us, Lord, if we unwittingly share in the conditions or in a system that perpetuates injustice.

Show us how we can serve your children
and make your love practical
by washing their feet.

Mother Teresa, India

Faith Is What Will Save Us!

Dear God,

please give us wisdom in this time of rash action.

Give us help in conquering evil, but not in destroying good.

May we see that all people are equal,

and that our suffering here is like suffering everywhere.

Give us your loving embrace in this time of loss.

Shelter in your kingdom those who have perished.

Let the world be brought together in love, not vengeance—

let your children see what a difference they can make!

Most of all, fill our hearts with faith,

for that is what will save us. Amen.

Tess, U.S.A.

Make Amends for Us, Lord!

Lord Jesus, you are the source of peace. You alone can give true peace to our hearts and to our troubled world. We humbly come before you at this particular moment, knowing that by ourselves we can do nothing to restore peace unless you go before us making amends where we have destroyed.

This is our peace prayer from Tanzania, united with the entire world's prayer and with people of good will everywhere who are seeking and working for peace.

Guided by the Holy Spirit, we may overcome our selfishness and value the precious gift of life that you have given freely to all of us to enjoy in this world until we return to you. Amen.

Annie, Tanzania

Salaam

In the name of Allah, Most Gracious, Most Merciful:
God, you are peace
and peace is from you.
Please let us live in peace.

Amin Chanaa, Palestine

Our Refuge in Terror

Almighty, ever-living God,

we beg you to restore peace in the world.

Look with kindness on our brothers and sisters

who are suffering because of war.

Turn their tears into joy,

strengthen their hearts with faith,

and be their refuge during this time of terror.

It is hard to acknowledge your presence in an unstable country,

but with you, Lord, nothing is impossible.

Heavenly Father, grant us peace and unity.

We pray this through the name of Jesus Christ our Lord. Amen.

Ninsiima Anna, Uganda

Give Me Strength for Each Day

Please, Lord,
remove any hatred from my heart.
Help me to continue each day
to do the work you have given me:
to be a mother, a sister, a friend, a nurse.
I may not be able to help in great ways,
but give me the strength to go through each day
fixing lunches, helping with homework,
answering questions from co-workers and patients.
Let my heart not fill
with despair or complacency,
hatred or indifference.
Keep all of us in your light
during any dark days ahead. Amen.

Luann, U.S.A.

Ancient Peace Prayer

O Almighty!

Lead us from the false to the true!

From darkness to light!

From mortality to immortality!

O Almighty! May there be peace! Peace! Peace!

Someone praying in India

I Breathe God's Peace

"Peace, peace to the far and near," says the Lord, "and I will heal them"
(Is 57:19).

At dawn I sit before God in silent contemplation...a creature
meeting the Creator...the most sacred moments of my day.
Eyes closed, I ask to experience the Divine within me and around
me. I breathe, in and out, the PEACE that comes from God alone....
I send out PEACE to all people all over the world, chanting:

OM, SHANTI... SHANTI... SHANTI....
which means, PEACE... PEACE... PEACE....

At the end of my prayer, I slowly open my eyes saying:

May all human beings be happy!
May God unite everyone in love, unity, and peace.

Leela, India

Rebuild What Is Broken in Us

Almighty God of justice, peace, and love,
rebuild within us the broken bonds of truth,
sincerity, and equality.
Grant us, we pray, a change of heart
so that we may be genuinely committed
to a world where everyone shares the fruit of peace.

Lord, you who said, "I give you peace,"
make it true in our hearts, in our families,
in our workplaces, in our country, and in our world.

Lord, this is our heart's desire: to have peace, to live peace,
to share signs of peace, to have smiles of peace.
Let it be that whenever we meet injury and hatred,
we may sow love,
where there is struggle and striving,
let us step forward and speak of peace.
Peace! Peace! We cry peace! Peace is our hope. Amen.

Rosemary, Kenya

The Violence of Love

We have never preached violence,
except the violence of love,
which left Christ nailed to a cross;
the violence that we must each do to ourselves
to overcome our selfishness
and such cruel inequalities among us.

The violence we preach is not the violence of the sword,
the violence of hatred.
It is the violence of love,
of brotherhood,
the violence that wills to beat weapons
into sickles for work.

Oscar Romero, El Salvador

Allah the Merciful

It may be that Allah will grant love and friendship between you and those whom you now hold as enemies. For Allah has power over all things; and Allah is oft-forgiving, most merciful.

Qur'an 60:7

This Heavy Hour of War

God, look on your children with eyes of pity. Jesus said, "ask and you shall receive," and with this assurance in our hearts, we beg you to come to the aid of humanity. Tragedies have taken place—famine, hatred, mourning—Father, bring peace to your children!

Send your Holy Spirit on leaders of nations to enlighten and direct them in this heavy hour of war; help them to make the right decisions. Throughout this dear, vast land of ours—at once beautiful and barren—lay your hand on each of us and, together with national leaders, help us to offer peace to each other and peace to those who desire to join us in making this land a loving, joyful, and compassionate place. Amen.

Thecla, Australia

Sh'ma: Personal Declaration of Faith

Hear, O Israel—
the divine abounds everywhere
and dwells in everything;
the many are One.

Loving life
and its mysterious source,
with all my heart and all my spirit,
all my senses and all my strength,
I take upon myself and into myself these promises:
to care for the earth
and those who live upon it,
to pursue justice and peace,
to love kindness and compassion.
I will teach this to our children
throughout the passage of the day—
as I dwell at home and as I go on my journey,
from the time I rise until I fall asleep.
And may my actions

be faithful to my words
that our children's children
may live to know
that truth and kindness
have embraced,
peace and justice have kissed
and are one.

Marcia, U.S.A.

And I will grant peace in
the land, and you shall lie down,
and no one shall make you afraid.

Leviticus 26:6

What's Most Important

God, to me, the most important letter in the alphabet is F.
It's not a pretty letter, it's not the first letter of the alphabet or the
first letter of my name. It's kind of hidden between a suave vowel
and a stellar consonant. But everything that's important in my
life starts with this letter.

F is for my FAITH, which guides my actions every day.

F is for my FAMILY. I've been blessed with two beautiful sisters
and a mother who is my hero.

F is for the FRIENDS I live for every day and with whom I share
my deepest feelings.

F is for FORTUNE. No matter how big my problems seem,
I need to be thankful because I've been blessed with so much.

F is for FREEDOM, something that I've taken for granted until I was
reminded how precious it is.

God, as we try to persevere in these tiring, trying times, bring
our world the peace it needs to cultivate something else which
begins with F...our FUTURE. Amen.

Sean, U.S.A.

Our Over-Active World

As we gaze into the world today, there is so much violence
and terrorism. The world needs your peace:
the peace of a newborn child,
the peace of a new dawn,
the peace of a young chick under the wings of its mother.

We implore you, Lord, to shower your peace
on this over-active world.
Increase the number of peacemakers.
Lord, bring peace to the broken pieces,
bring peace to this restless world.
This we ask you through Christ your Son, Prince of Peace. Amen.

Vimala, India

Be Calmly Centered

God,

may we be deeply absorbed in your love and peace.

May we abhor any violence and evil, as you do,

and praise you for the goodness of your world.

May we be calmly centered so that anxiety and the compulsion

to grasp at superficial answers may disappear.

Please help our effort to let go of the harsh wounds

that have so deeply scarred us.

Help us to realize that it's time for healing to begin.

To a world drawn into the darkness of war,

may each one of us act with wisdom rather than revenge,

and become an instrument of peace, working against the injustice

and violence done to powerless people.

May we overcome the great power of evil by following the

example of Jesus, who committed his life to peace as he died on

the cross. Let us follow you, armed with peace and justice,

ready to pay any price.

Maria, Susanna, and Bona, Korea

The World Feels Unsafe

God our Father,
we stand at the threshold of a new era
of spiritual and ethical challenges
in our country and in the world.
We see all around us
increased levels of violence, corruption,
dangerous expressions of fundamentalism,
and a lack of genuine, sincere dialogue
among all national leaders.
We see the unchecked spread of AIDS,
the neglect and abuse of refugees,
the use of children in war, and other grave injustices,
which threaten the peace of the world.
Lord Jesus, we beg you—give us peace.

Fidelis, Uganda

To the God of Love and Compassion

God,

you created us and know all our potentials and limitations.

You see how we have become so divided

because of race, religion, and culture.

Among us, and even within us, we live in a divided world.

Please, God, enlighten us, so we can build up lasting unity

among all peoples.

In our efforts for world peace,

help us to concentrate more on our similarities

than on those things that keep us apart.

O God,

you came to earth to show us the way of life.

Please, God, enfold all peoples in your love.

May they experience deeply the grace of your redemption now,

before we destroy all that has been created and sustained by such

love and compassion.

Maria Cruz, Spain

Transform Hatred

Heavenly Father,
please hold out your hand to anyone who is suffering
from loss due to terrorist attacks. Please unite them with your
Son's suffering on the cross. Please have mercy on them,
have mercy on us all.

Father, I ask you to transform any hatred those who are suffering
may feel in their hearts; show them your love as you have showed
it to others. I ask this through Christ our Lord. Amen.

Lydia, Singapore

We Have Nowhere Else to Turn

Heavenly Father, we turn to you in the midst of our tragedy
and suffering. We have nowhere else to turn, for you alone
are the source of truth and love.

Do not allow us to fall into the pit of bitterness, hatred,
and vengeance. Lift us from the depths of our grief and sorrow.

Help us to see that you are always with us, even in the midst
of impenetrable darkness. For nothing can separate us
from your love.

Keep and watch over us, the sheep of your flock. Amen.

Thomas, U.S.A.

We Reel from Terror

God,

the soul of the world yearns for peace even as it reels after terror. No person, no state, no nation today is free from the clutches of violence and its vicious circle of hatred, revenge, and more violence. Today, innocent lives pay the price for the world's evils.

Have mercy, O God! We lift up to you the leaders of all nations, all terrorist organizations, all groups and individuals who are determined to resort to violence. Remove from every heart all harshness, all egoism, all discord. Enkindle, instead, the longing for peace and the need to safeguard life. Multiply every effort made toward healing and forgiveness.

Lord, may everyone aspire to be what you want us to be— children of peace who work for peace. Amen.

Suesan, India

Look Within...

The hunger, thirst, and utter misery of poor nations is a tragedy. But the greater tragedy is that there are nations of the world that are oblivious to the enslavement and exploitation of these poor nations.

F. X. Nguyen Van Thuan, Vietnam

Prayer of Confession

Lord, Jesus Christ, you are the way of peace.
Come into the brokenness of our lives
and our world with your healing love.
Help us to be willing to bow before you
in true repentance,
and to bow to one another in real forgiveness.
By the fire of your Holy Spirit,
melt our hard hearts,
consume the pride and prejudice
that separate us.
Fill us, O Lord, with your love
which casts out our fears,
and draws us together in the unity
that you call us to share as God's people. Amen.

Someone praying in Northern Ireland

I am for peace…

Psalm 120:7

Litany of Contradictory Things

People of God who wound and heal:
let them grow together.

Arabs and Jews in Palestine:
let them grow together.

Greeks and Turks of the Balkans:
let them grow together.

Catholics and Protestants of Northern Ireland:
let them grow together.

Pros and Contras of Central America:
let them grow together.

Immigrants and Native Americans:
let them grow together.

Blacks and whites of South Africa:
let them grow together.

Sikhs and Hindus of India:
let them grow together.

Revolutionaries and reactionaries:
let them grow together.

Rich and poor, humble and haughty:
let them grow together.

Contemplation and action:
let them grow together.

Wisdom of the East and West:
let them grow together.

All the seasons of one's life:
let them grow together.

Michael, U.S.A.

"Yes"

Peace
is only found
in yes.

Anthony de Mello, India

Comfort Refugees

God of all races, deliver us from prejudice, greed, and pride,
which deny fullness of life to our neighbors.
Be with all victims of racial prejudice,
and with those who are driven from their land
and whose way of life is destroyed.
Give us all hope and courage
as we seek the good of your people everywhere.

   Someone praying in Brazil

Christ Is Now!

Some want to keep a gospel so disembodied
that it doesn't get involved at all
in the world it must save.
Christ is now in history.
Christ is in the womb of the people.
Christ is now bringing about
the new heavens and the new earth.

Oscar Romero, El Salvador

Co-Creators

Who brings about peace
is called
the companion of God
in the work of creation.

Jewish proverb

Embracing the Risks

Help us, good Lord,
to take on in your name
the risks involved
in the struggle for peace and justice.

Someone praying in France

The Point of Crisis

Spirit of truth and judgment,
who alone can exorcize
the powers that grip our world,
at the point of crisis
give us your discernment
that we may accurately name what is evil
and know the way that leads to peace,
through Jesus Christ. Amen.

Janet, United Kingdom

Hear My Voice!

To you, Creator of nature and humanity,
hear my voice, for it is the voice of victims of all wars and
violence among individuals and nations.

Hear my voice, for it is the voice of all children who suffer and
will suffer when people put their faith in weapons and war.

Hear my voice when I beg you to instill into the hearts of all
human beings the wisdom of peace, the strength of justice,
and the joy of fellowship.

Hear my voice, for I speak for the multitudes in every
country and every period of history who do not want war
and are ready to walk the road of peace.

Hear my voice, and grant insight and strength so that we
may always respond to hatred with love, to injustice with
total dedication to justice, to need with the sharing of self,
to war with peace.

O God, hear my voice, and grant unto the world
your everlasting peace.

Prayer of Pope John Paul II at Hiroshima

O God of Justice and Joy

O God of justice and joy
may the goods we bring
to the market place
bring life
and health
and well being
to all who trade there.

Teach us
to refuse a bargain
that leaves others
without the means of life.
May our world
trade not in human lives
but so that all may live. Amen.

Someone praying in the United Kingdom

God, help me to be a person who radiates your peace. May I show your love to those I live with and rub shoulders with each day,

> saying a kind word,
> giving in,
> going out of my way,
> being selfless instead of self-centered.

By your grace and power, O God, I believe you can use these small acts to touch hearts in my family, community, country, and world. May your grace multiply goodness and bring peace to all the earth. Amen.

Diane, U.S.A.

Overturn the Greed!

Angry Jesus,
as of old when you entered into that temple market
casting out the merchants and money changers,
enter now into the markets of our modern world.
Throw out of them all that is unworthy, unjust, and self-seeking
and direct the market-forces of the world
in the ways of justice, plenty, and peace,
for your tender mercy's sake. Amen.

Author Unknown

Unity of Life

Deliver us, O God,
from politics without principles,
from wealth without work,
from pleasure without conscience,
from knowledge without character,
from commerce without morality,
from worship without sacrifice,
and from science without humanity. Amen.

   Someone praying in India

Our Hearts Cry out "Why?"

Father,

we come before you with humble and contrite hearts...hearts that ache, cry out, and ask *why?*

See the pain, hurt, and agony that we are feeling; in your divine goodness and unfathomable mercy, bless families, friends, co-workers, and those who offer help. Fill them with your healing power of peace, solace, love, and mercy.

In the midst of darkness, let your light shine. Draw all to you by the power of your Holy Spirit. Help us, dear Lord, to be candles of light in this dark world. Help us to be the channels of your healing power so that, joined as one, we can praise, honor, and give glory to you, Father. With confidence, we call you Abba! Amen.

Michelle, U.S.A.

Act Rightly Before Your God

Loose the bonds of injustice,
share your bread with the hungry,
bring the homeless into your house.
Then you shall be like a watered garden,
like a spring of water
whose waters never fail.

Isaiah 58:6–7, 11

Struggling Together

All barriers of race and religion can be overcome
when people work together in common endeavors,
based on love and compassion.

Aung San Suu Kyi, Myanmar

Enhancing Freedom

I am not truly free if I am taking away someone else's freedom, just as surely as I am not free when my freedom is taken from me…to be free is not merely to cast off one's chains, but to live in a way that respects and enhances the freedom of others.

Nelson Mandela, South Africa

Pray Tirelessly

We must pray without tiring, for the salvation of humanity does not depend on material success or on science. Neither does it depend on arms and human industries, but on Jesus alone.

Saint Frances Cabrini

Peace Prayer of St. Francis

Lord, make me an instrument of your peace.

Where there is hatred...let me sow love.

Where there is injury...pardon.

Where there is discord...unity.

Where there is doubt...faith.

Where there is error...truth.

Where there is despair...hope.

Where there is sadness...joy.

Where there is darkness...light.

O Divine Master, grant that I may not so much seek

to be consoled...as to console,

to be understood...as to understand,

to be loved...as to love.

For it is in giving...that we receive.

It is in pardoning...that we are pardoned.

It is in dying...that we are born to eternal life.

As prayed by Cardinal Joseph Bernardin

Our Cornerstone of Peace

Almighty God,

the Roaring Thunder that splits mighty trees,

all-seeing Lord,

do not hesitate to respond to our call.

You are the cornerstone of peace.

African prayer

Sustain Our Search for Peace

Dear God, in this very difficult time, may we all unite in a search for your peace. You have been very patient with us, despite our wanderings, and you long for us all to reach out and touch your hand through prayer. Help and sustain us, not only now in our time of distress, but all the way as we journey back to you.

Ken, U.S.A.

Growing in Peace

O Great Spirit,

give us the wisdom to teach our children to love, to respect,

and to be kind to each other

so that they may grow with peace in mind.

Let us learn to share all good things

that you provide for us on this earth. Amen.

Native American prayer

Peace Unto Us All

We think of thee, worship thee, bow to thee as the Creator of this universe; we seek refuge in thee, the truth, our only support. Thou art the ruler, the barge in this ocean of endless births and deaths.

In the name of Allah, the Beneficent, the Merciful:

> Praise be to the Lord of the universe who has created us and made us into tribes and nations. Give us wisdom that we may know each other and not despise all things. We shall abide by thy peace. And, we shall remember the servants of God that those who walk on this earth in humility and, when we address them, we shall say peace unto us all.
>
> Islamic peace prayer

Unshakeable Faith

I still believe, in spite of everything, that people are really good inside.

Anne Frank, Netherlands

I'm Angry, God!

God, I feel angry. This morning, with Psalm 102, I prayed, "The children of your servants shall live secure." So many people who serve you do *not* dwell secure, and neither do their children. I glance at the newspaper. I see the poverty, the wars, the enslavement of the human person. I see the immense helplessness that so many people experience in the face of unjust systems. And I say to you, "What's happening to their prayers, God? Are you making of them a carpet for your feet? These people need for you to lean down from heaven. It is enough! It is enough, God!"

In the shadows, I seem to see God leaning from heaven, a sorrowing, desperate parent, and God repeats to the human race my own agonizing cry, "It is enough! How long must I wait for you to put on the mind of Christ? How long must I wait for you to live in my image? What are you doing with the prayers of your brothers and sisters? Are you making them into plush carpets for your own feet to rest on?"

What are we doing to the image of God in one another?

Macrina, U.S.A.

A Justice Fired with Love

Give us, Father, a vision of your world
as love would make it;
a world whose benefits are shared
so that everyone can enjoy them;
a world whose different people and cultures
live with tolerance and mutual respect;
a world where peace is built with justice,
and justice is fired with love;
and give us the courage to build it,
through Jesus Christ our Lord.

Someone praying in Guatemala

A harvest of righteousness
is sown in peace
for those who make peace.

James 3:18

Sustain Our Hope

Father,
as we offer you the deaths of those attacked by violence,
we remember your Chosen People in the desert.
When they were struck by serpents,
Moses made a bronze serpent for them to look upon
and be healed.
As we now look upon what has struck us,
we also need healing.
Give us faith, sustain our hope,
and grant us a share in your mercy.

Gretchen, U.S.A.

Open Us, O Lord

Lord, open our eyes,

that we may see you in our brothers and sisters.

Lord, open our ears,

that we may hear the cries from the hungry, the cold,

the frightened, the oppressed.

Lord, open our hands,

that we may reach out to all who are in need.

Lord, open our hearts,

that we may love each other as you love us.

Someone praying in Canada

An Honest Plea

Dear and loving God:
I despise violence and prejudice.
Please do not let me become
what I hate!

John, U.S.A.

For Victims Everywhere

We pray for those in the world who have forgotten that all people are made in your image and likeness and are of equal worth in your eyes; for those who suffer because of racial oppression and social injustice; for those who struggle for human dignity; for those who have lost their hope for the future.

We pray for the needy and suffering in the world; for the hungry and thirsty; for the homeless; for the unemployed and the unemployable; for the victims of alcoholism; for the victims of drug addiction; for the sick, in mind or body; for the lonely and the elderly.

We pray for all parents, that they may give their children the love and guidance which will help them to find the right way in life; for all children without parents; for young people, that they may find hope for the future; for peace between nations and good will among all people.

Lord, hear us!

Someone praying in Sweden

The Big Picture

An individual has not started living until he or she can rise above the narrow confines of his or her individualistic concerns to the broader concerns of all humanity.

Martin Luther King, Jr., U.S.A.

Sincerity

Many who are indignant about injustices are only indignant when the injustices are being inflicted on them. Their indignation is skin-deep.

Etty Hillesum, Netherlands

Let Us Be Light

We ask you, merciful Father,
that we may treat one another with great sensitivity,
always wishing the best for each other.
Lord, grant that I may be a bearer of light, not of darkness.
Let me always witness to love and unity.
May your Spirit show each of us
the path that leads toward an encounter with you. Amen.

Noe, El Salvador

Steadfast

Lord, our faith has been shaken.
Still, we stand before you today and say:
We believe. We believe. Amen.

Louis, U.S.A.

Our Hurting World

God—
heart ripped apart—
walking in circles
looking for loved ones—
photos in hand.
Days passing slowly—
one then another.
Hope's still alive—
candles grow dimmer.
I'm praying for the hurting—
praying for the world.

Lois, U.S.A.

Change

You must be the change you wish to see in the world.

Mahatma Gandhi, India

Break Down the Walls That Divide Us

Lord God, you have created the earth from end to end, and in you there is no distinction of race, color, class, or language, but in you all are one. We ask you to break down the walls which divide us so that we may work together with one mind and heart, with one another and with you. We ask this in Jesus' name. Amen.

Anglican reading

Our Lives Are in Your Hands

Almighty God,
we come before you, conscious as always that our lives
and our destinies are in your hands.

God of mercies,
we beg you to receive into a place of refreshment, light, and
peace, the souls of any who have died tragically. We pray that
your gentle hand of compassion may fall upon all those
who weep and mourn over their loved ones.

God of righteousness,
we ask that you fill us with courage, with prudence, and with a
renewed commitment to defend the blessings of freedom.

God of justice,
as we mourn, may we resolve before you, the Author of Life,
that the dead shall not have died in vain. We pray that,
through their sacrifice and the united action of humanity,
the world is made a safer, saner, nobler place. Amen.

George, U.S.A.

Bridging the Gap

How can I pray for peace when I am not at peace?
I can't relax.
I want to keep moving, to finish my work—
for tomorrow may never come.
I need peace, just a little peace.
I have to quiet down,
to be still,
and allow things to happen
without the desire to change anything
except my ability to be at peace.

I pray that the media will take responsibility for what it reports,
and broadcast the truth that might bridge the gap
between West and East.
I pray that the media will expose the hidden agenda
of those who are anti-life and anti-peace,
so that all nations will join together
to forge a new world in peace and justice. Amen.

Athens, Pakistan

The Energy of God

Lord,

thank you for filling my life with vibrant energy.

Because energy can be the source of peace and love, or of hatred
and violence, I ask you, Holy Spirit, to guide me in using
my energies and gifts to spread love and peace in the world.
Do not allow me to contribute to the chaos in the world
by using my energies in anger or hatred—with this kind of
energy, only the push of a button is enough for disaster.
Instead, let me offer peace to the world—let peace
begin with me. Amen.

An Mei, China

Your Kingdom Come

Father,
we are sad.
So many people live in countries
with poverty and violence,
but without any hope.
Please,
send us your Spirit of truth and love,
that we may walk
the path of humanity and freedom *together.*
May your kingdom come.

Gabriela, Germany

Through Our Hands

Make us worthy, Lord, to serve our neighbors
throughout the world
who live and die in poverty and hunger.
Give them, through our hands, this day
their daily bread,
and by our understanding love,
give peace and joy.

Mother Teresa, India

The Reign of Peace

It's sad that each generation
seems to have its own September 11.
May God's peace reign some day soon
on this broken planet.
May God have mercy
on all those who have died tragically.
And may the people of this world realize
that death and violence
are never a solution to our problems. Amen.

Michael, U.S.A.

A New Prayer of St. Francis

Lord Jesus, give us an awareness
of the massive forces threatening our world.

Where there is armed conflict,
let us stretch out our arms to our brothers and sisters.

Where there is abundance,
let there be simple lifestyles and sharing.

Where there is poverty,
let there be dignity and constant striving for justice.

Where there is selfish ambition,
let there be humble service.

Where there is injustice,
let there be atonement.

Where there is despair,
let there be hope in the Good News.

Where there are wounds of division,
let there be unity and wholeness.

Help us to be committed to the building of your kingdom,
not seeking to be cared for, but to care;
not expecting to be served, but to serve others;
not desiring material security,
but placing our security in your love.

For it is only in loving imitation of you, Lord,
that we can discover the healing springs of life
to bring about new birth on our earth
and hope for the world. Amen.

Melba Grace, Philippines

Remove the Dark Clouds of War

Eternal, loving Father,
you created the world out of chaos,
and today we have taken your world back into chaos.
Yes, Father,
our world is hurting, our world is in pain…
and it seems to increase every day!
Today, more than ever, we want to do good,
but the power of evil seems greater than us, O Lord.
Take away the dark clouds of imminent war!
Heal the wounds we have inflicted
on our neighboring countries
and those inflicted on us!
We long for peace in our country.
Lord, we long for peace in the world. Amen.

Elsy, India

Be Children of God

Blessed are the peacemakers, for they will be called children of God. But I say to you, love your enemies and pray for those who persecute you. If anyone strikes you on the right cheek, turn the other also; and if anyone wants to sue you and take your coat, give your cloak as well. Give to everyone who begs from you, and do not refuse anyone who wants to borrow from you. In everything do to others as you would have them do to you.

Matthew 5:9, 44, 39–40, 42; 7:12

We Pray Together

Benevolent Lord,
Creator and Sustainer of us all,
hear your children in times of unbearable pain.
Only you can heal our wounds and ease our suffering.
Help us, and people throughout the world,
to comprehend that *we are all your children*.

As one great, united world, we are a beautiful mosaic of peoples
of all colors, races, creeds, and cultural traditions.
Guide us to live in harmony,
respectful of each other's human dignity.
May your light illumine all humanity as we pray together:

> Our Father, who art in heaven, hallowed be thy name. Thy
> kingdom come; thy will be done on earth as it is in heaven.
> Give us this day our daily bread; and forgive us our trespasses
> as we forgive those who trespass against us; and lead us not
> into temptation, but deliver us from evil. Amen.

Methodios, Greece

Never Give Up the Search

God, you are the God of life.
Transform us in the depths of our hearts
into people through whom your peace
is carried out into your world.

Send your Spirit into the hearts of those
who are captured in the net of violence,
be it as perpetrators or as victims,
and let us never give up the search
for the chance to talk to them.

Someone praying in Croatia

Jewish Blessing of Peace

Eternal wellspring of peace,
may we be drenched with the longing for peace
that we may give ourselves over
as the earth to the rain, to the dew,
until peace overflows our lives
as living waters overflow the seas.

Marcia, U.S.A.

Despite the Chaos

Dear God,

may you instill in your children a sense of your peace,

so that in all the chaos, within and without,

we may always know your peace. Amen.

Karen, Singapore

Peace in Any Language

God, all humanity cries out to you:

Give us peace, pax, paix, pace, shalom, amani...
  Peace in our families and peace among families,
  peace in each country and peace among countries,
  peace in each continent and peace among continents,
  peace in each religion and peace among different religions,
  for we are all your children.

Give us peace, pax, pace, paix, shalom, amani...
  Peace in our minds,
  peace in our words,
  peace in our attitudes,
  peace in our hearts,
  peace in our thoughts,
  peace in our actions.
  Make peace become our behavior.

Give us peace, pax, pace, paix, shalom, amani...
  Inspire those in power:

to act justly in sharing wealth,

to govern with love,

to resolve problems by dialogue,

to respect human rights,

to promote the whole human being.

Give us peace, pax, pace, paix, shalom, amani…. Amen.

Augustine, Congo

Seek peace and pursue it.

1 Peter 3:11

Walking in the Light

They shall beat their swords into plowshares, and their spears into pruning hooks; nation shall not lift up sword against nation, neither shall they learn war any more. O house of Jacob, come let us walk in the light of the Lord.

Isaiah 2:4–5

Equation

If you want peace, work for justice.

Pope Paul VI

Fill Your Heart

Finally, beloved, whatever is true, whatever is honorable,
whatever is just, whatever is pure...if there is anything
worthy of praise, think about these things.
And the God of peace will be with you.

Philippians 4:8–9

Prayers

Music

Photos

Page 11: United Nations PS/AB

Pages 30, 51, 81: Daughters of St. Paul

Page 95: Mary Emmanuel Alves, FSP

Pages 122, 150: Rev. Msgr. Russell Terra

Pauline
BOOKS & MEDIA

The Daughters of St. Paul operate book and media centers at the following addresses. Visit, call or write the one nearest you today, or find us on the World Wide Web, www.pauline.org

CALIFORNIA
3908 Sepulveda Blvd, Culver City, CA 90230   310-397-8676

5945 Balboa Avenue, San Diego, CA 92111   858-565-9181

46 Geary Street, San Francisco, CA 94108   415-781-5180

FLORIDA
145 S.W. 107th Avenue, Miami, FL 33174   305-559-6715

HAWAII
1143 Bishop Street, Honolulu, HI 96813   808-521-2731

Neighbor Islands call: 800-259-8463

ILLINOIS
172 North Michigan Avenue, Chicago, IL 60601   312-346-4228

LOUISIANA
4403 Veterans Blvd, Metairie, LA 70006   504-887-7631

MASSACHUSETTS
Rte. 1, 885 Providence Hwy, Dedham, MA 02026 781-326-5385

MISSOURI
9804 Watson Road, St. Louis, MO 63126   314-965-3512

NEW JERSEY
561 U.S. Route 1, Wick Plaza, Edison, NJ 08817 732-572-1200

NEW YORK
150 East 52nd Street, New York, NY 10022   212-754-1110

78 Fort Place, Staten Island, NY 10301   718-447-5071

OHIO
2105 Ontario Street, Cleveland, OH 44115   216-621-9427

PENNSYLVANIA
9171-A Roosevelt Blvd, Philadelphia, PA 19114   215-676-9494

SOUTH CAROLINA
243 King Street, Charleston, SC 29401   843-577-0175

TENNESSEE
4811 Poplar Avenue, Memphis, TN 38117   901-761-2987

TEXAS
114 Main Plaza, San Antonio, TX 78205   210-224-8101

VIRGINIA
1025 King Street, Alexandria, VA 22314   703-549-3806

CANADA
3022 Dufferin Street, Toronto, Ontario, Canada M6B 3T5 416-781-9131

1155 Yonge Street, Toronto, Ontario, Canada M4T 1W2 416-934-3440

¡También somos su fuente para libros, videos y música en español!